Life on Lisbon Ridge

Donald Wile

Copyright © 2024 Donald Wile
All rights reserved
First Edition

Fulton Books
Meadville, PA

Published by Fulton Books 2024

ISBN 979-8-89427-708-0 (paperback)
ISBN 979-8-89427-709-7 (digital)

Printed in the United States of America

To my wife and best friend, Jane.
One lifetime is not enough to show
you how much I love you.

FOREWORD

Lisbon Falls, Maine, one of the boroughs of the town of Lisbon, in 1954, was a small town of around six thousand people. It lies in Androscoggin County, almost exactly halfway between Portland, Augusta, Lewiston, and Brunswick. One of the books written about Lisbon states that the town of Lisbon was the jewel of Androscoggin County.

All of these stories in this book are real memories that I have been able to bring to mind. After the fire, I found I couldn't remember any Christmastimes or Thanksgivings. Being only nine years old at the time, things like a fire delete younger memories. I use that word for lack of a better one.

After I got married and my husband and I had made many friends, we would have dinner parties, and Don would ask me to tell some of my memories to our guests. Most were humorous, and our friends loved them.

As you can see, Don wrote them down and finally got them into book form. It took many years to collect them.

I hope you will enjoy them.

Jane Kiszonak Wile
June 4, 2020

CHAPTER 1

Mom and Dad were married in 1937. For a short time, they lived in a little house on Upper Main Street. Mom called it her dollhouse. It wasn't long before they moved to the top of High Street Hill, across from the cemetery. Dad worked, and Mom stayed home. Newlywed life seemed to agree with them both. In 1939, Mom had her first child, a girl she named Joan. At that time, Dad was selling insurance, but when war was declared, Dad joined the army. Mom and Joan lived there until Dad came home from the war.

Dad wanted to be a farmer, so he bought cows and chickens and pigs. Of course, he had to have a tractor and other equipment. Mom and Dad did okay with the farm, but it was hard work because they had to haul the water from the house to the barn. There was no water piped into the barn at that time.

In 1954, Mom had twins. She named us Jim and Jane. Joan was away at Kents Hill in Readfield and was absolutely surprised to see she had a new brother and sister. She was fifteen at the time. Mom and Dad had babies along with the livestock to care for.

My brother and I grew up in Lisbon Falls, Maine. At that time, the town was full of the sounds of everyday life. People from all over the world came to this little place in the state to find work and make a living. People from Canada, Germany, Russia, Czechoslovakia, and Eastern Europe came here to work in the mills or start up their own businesses.

The older townspeople tell of the tribe of Native Americans who lived here before. Their name for this area was "the place of many fishes" because they would catch all they could eat while fishing from the rocks on the riverbank.

We have few thunderstorms, and they only reach us if they follow the river down the valley; otherwise, the ridges are high enough that the storms are deflected to the north or south of us.

My brother and I grew up on what was called Lisbon Ridge. It is the highest point of land in Androscoggin County, Maine. We were on a farm just about a mile north. Looking a little northwest, we could see Mount Washington in New Hampshire. Now the view is blocked by years of tree growth.

Right from the start, we were the cutest little monsters around. Being early, we were small, but we also had the strength to survive. Mom and Dad worked hard to keep us warm and fed along with running their farm. In the summer, Mom would lay us on a blanket in the sun with nothing on. We need the sun to make vitamin D in our skin.

When I and my brother came along, the work-load increased because we needed a lot of care. Every so often, a friend of Mom's would come up to the farm and give Mom a rest, but most of the time, it was just her. Dad worked in a few different jobs in town. He taught school and coached athletics at LHS before he went into the army, and when he returned home, he taught and held the principal's position at the same school.

Dad had a great love for the town of Lisbon. Even though he worked all day, he was a member of almost every club that was formed in town. The clubs he belonged to were the Lower Club, the Upper Club, the Left-Hand Club, the Lobster Club, the Cribbage Club, and the Fish and Game Association. If he wasn't chairman of these clubs, he held an important position in them. Later in his life, he worked for the Farnsworth and Worumbo mills as a supervisor. He also worked for the town as road commissioner and finally was elected to selectman.

All the time Dad worked, Mom was at the farm taking care of us. We would get up in the morning, have breakfast, and then Mom would send us outside to play. She would always tell us to stay near the house and not to go into the fields. Being the adventurous little kids we were, she didn't want us to get lost.

One winter, when Jim and I were older (four or five), Jim decided he would remove a few of the barn windows with his shovel. The snow was just high enough against the barn so he could reach them. Dad didn't yell at us, and as I said, being twins, it was understood that if one was doing something they weren't supposed to, the other one was just as guilty, so you might as well join in. Being twins was a burden sometimes. All in all, we were well-behaved and didn't get into much trouble. There wasn't much to do on the farm in winter, but we still had the whole one hundred acres to explore. We couldn't go very far from the house; the snow on the ridge usually was higher than our heads in places. The days dragged on and on, and when they started to get warmer, we couldn't wait for spring.

Spring was the time of year when life on the farm started to get interesting. As the snow melted and the days warmed up, we were able to go out and play. We explored as much of the farm as we were allowed. Dad always had a garden. He would plant beans and carrots, tomatoes and peas. It was my and my brother's job to take care of the garden. It was supposed to give us something to do. Dad had an apple orchard not too far from the house, and my brother and I would spend part of the day exploring the trees and surrounding fields.

Summers were fun on the farm. The days were warm, and it was fun just to run down into the fields behind the house. We loved to dig in the ground and look for worms. We also played in the barn. There were no animals, so we explored the building to every corner. The barn swallows would fly at us whenever we went inside.

Mom and Dad had plenty of cats on the farm. A couple were ours, but some were from other farms and had wandered into the barn when they were cold and decided to take up residence. They lived in the barn and took over an old sleigh that Dad had kept. They weren't really pets, as Mom wouldn't let us bring any into the house, but we were allowed to feed them, so they stayed around. They would also find their food by reducing the number of mice found around the farm. Of course, cats are very fruitful, and in no time at all, there were too many. Dad had to reduce the population. He never said anything, but all of a sudden, there were fewer.

There was one day that I got a scare. I was down at the end of the field, standing at the tree line, when I heard something very big moving through the trees. I knew we had deer in the woods behind the house. I had seen them eating the apples from the old trees. This sounded a lot bigger than a deer, though. Listening very hard and looking in every direction at once, I started to enter the tree line. I had just taken a step when this big old moose came at me. He gave out one big snort, and I ran as fast as I could out into the field with the moose right behind me. Of course, the moose was much faster than I was, but I reached a tree in time to climb it. That moose just kept going back into the woods, and I didn't wait very long before I climbed down and ran back to the house.

Everyone said we were cute and busy children at the age of six. I suppose so. We did have a few small experiences, especially when Jim was given a balsa wood airplane. I had long hair then. I was always sitting on it. Well, Jim thought it would be funny to wind up the propeller and stick it into my hair. It took Mom cutting my hair real short to get the propeller out. I had short hair for a long time after that.

We had relatives in the next town, and when the ones from New Jersey came up, we went to visit them. We all got together in the game room, and my brother and I would watch as the grown-ups played penny-ante poker. We weren't allowed to play then. We had to grow a little before they would let us.

And of course, when people from away come to Maine, there has to be the ever-popular lobster feed. Back then, the lobsters were relatively inexpensive, and you could buy quite a few for a decent price. Clams and corn on the cob rounded out the meal, and everyone had a wonderful time. Boy, those are great memories.

All too soon, vacation time was over, and my relatives had to return to their homes. It was the Sunday before school started, and my brother and I had to be up at five in the morning to catch the bus.

CHAPTER 2

In the fall, when the leaves turned color and the apple trees were dropping apples, Jim and I would sit quietly at dusk and watch the deer come out to eat at the trees. They would wander around, and sometimes, when we were inside, they would come up to the house and even look into the back bedroom window. Many a time, Mom would yell because she would see something looking at her through the window. When she realized what it was, she would go out and scare the deer away. Jim and I always laughed at that.

Fall was, and still is, my favorite time of year. I love the colors and the smell of the leaves that have already fallen. It's that time of year that brings memories of warm days and cool nights, of baking in the kitchen, picking what few apples were left on the trees, and having family close as we got ready for the winter. Early in the evening, just after supper, Dad would rake a small pile of leaves into the garden where the ground was bare, and we would burn a small amount. I loved the smell of burning leaves, and it was nice just spending time with Dad, as he was always busy doing something down in town.

On the weekends, when hunting season came around, Dad would take me down into the woodlot, and I would follow him as he hunted for rabbits. He would tell me to be very quiet, but as I loved the animals so much, I just couldn't. Finally, he would only take me on Sundays. Hunting wasn't allowed on Sundays back then. I did remember to take my camera along on a Sunday and was able to take a picture of Dad carrying his rifle through the woods. Sometimes, Dad would let Jim and me ride in the trunk of the car down to the tree line. There, we would sit and watch the trees as Dad shone the car lights into the woods. We would see the eyes of the animals shine back at us.

Winter was a trial for all of us on the farm. The weather was so cold that some days we didn't leave the house. The snow would pile up against the house and barn, almost to the windows. But on the days we could go out, there was sliding and snow angels and all sorts of other things we could do. Out behind the upper field, there was a small pond that would freeze over. It was there that my brother and I learned to skate. Our friends would come over, and we would spend the afternoon skating until it was time for supper. One winter, there was a small ice storm, and the snow was covered with such a hard crust we could skate on it. It was a lot of fun skating all over the fields that winter.

One day, Mom and Dad decided to have a time by themselves. My sister happened to be home that evening, and Mom asked her to sit with us. They got ready, and before they left, they said they would be home early. I supposed we were not the perfect children people thought we were because when Mom and Dad got home, they found my sister sitting in the playpen knitting and my brother and I had the run of the house.

Another time, my sister was taking care of us, and I think she was trying to tire us out because she kept sending us upstairs to retrieve some things she needed and would give us a penny for each trip up the stairs we took. I think it was her way of tiring us out so we would go to bed.

The last time Mom asked my sister to sit with us, we misbehaved so badly she drove Jim under the big bed. He stayed there until he fell asleep. When Mom and Dad got home, they asked where Jim was. My sister said he was under the bed and had fallen asleep. Mom looked under the bed, found Jim sleeping, and decided he would come out when he woke up. From that moment on, Mom never let anyone babysit us.

CHAPTER 3

Another day of excitement came when my sister was getting married. Jim was going to be ring bearer, and I was the flower girl. The day was proceeding smoothly, and the groom's parents had arrived on the farm. Jim and I were dressed in our good clothes and were being unusually quiet when the mother-in-law asked what we thought about our sister getting married. We both, at the same time, turned to Mrs. Wheeler and said, "She's our sister?" My sister was fifteen years older than us, and we never knew to ask Mom about the girl who came to the farm every summer and stayed until fall. Anyway, we were quiet and trying to stay out of the way, when Mrs. Wheeler hurried into the room to ask Mom why she had let Jim hold the pillow that had the rings on it. She had been outside with the other kids, who belonged to friends of Mom and Dad, when she noticed that one of the rings was missing from the pillow. She spent about a half hour on her knees looking for the lost ring. Gravel driveways do wonders on nylon stock-ings; both knees were showing through. Mom was wonderful. She quietly explained that the rings on the pillow were not real rings but just costume jewelry. Mrs. Wheeler attended the wedding anyway.

After we had returned home, Mom sat us down and explained to us that the girl was our sister, who attended college and came home every summer.

When we turned seven or eight, Mom and Dad bought us a swing set. Back in those days, a swing was a length of stout rope with both ends tied to a convenient tree limb. Next, there was a board notched to fit the rope—that was the seat. When you sat on the seat and had your brother or friend push you, it felt like you could fly. Also, if there was a barn, then the rope would be tied to a large beam. The swing in the barn was much more popular because the weather didn't affect our playtime. As time went on, swings were made of iron, then steel pipes were welded together. The pipes were then set in cement in the ground so the person swinging wouldn't be able to tip the swing over. When aluminum became feasible, swings could be made in sets that could be put together by Mom and Dad. That was the kind that my parents brought home for us.

It was the kind made of pipes and had chains hooked to the seats. We would spend the whole day on that swing sometimes, and when we learned to climb up on it, that opened up many new possibilities. We found if we yelled into the big pipe on top, it made a most interesting sound. Mom, being in the house and doing her chores, didn't hear us at all.

One day, Dad was visiting a friend down the road from our farm. He and his friend were standing outside and talking when they heard a sound they had never heard before. Not seeing anything unusual, they kept talking until Dad left for home. When he drove up the driveway, he saw Jim and me on our swing yelling through the pipe. He said nothing and went into the house. Mom came out and called us into supper. Dad asked us if we had done anything interesting that day. We told him we had spent the day swinging.

The next morning, we jumped out of bed, got dressed, rushed through breakfast, and ran out the door, ready for another day on the swing. Up we climbed, but when we got to the top, we found that Dad had filled the ends of the pipe with cement. That took care of the strange sounds from the ridge. Now we had to find something else to entertain us.

Jim and I were looking forward to our birthday. Mom and Dad had bought us new bicycles that year. School had started, and we didn't have a lot of time to ride them. We did whenever we could. We could only ride them up and down the driveway, but that was okay; the driveway was a quarter of a mile long.

The year 1963 arrived very quietly. Being nine years old, we didn't watch much news on the TV. As school progressed through the last months before vacation, Jim and I were more involved in school matters. When Dad had the time, he would take us into town and let us stay at our grandparents' house for a few hours. We made friends all along the street and had fun for the few hours that Dad was in town. Anytime we were at our grandmother's house, we went looking for the friends we made on the next street. It was a good feeling not to have to walk a half mile to join in the many games we learned from our friends.

Jim and I were visiting our family at our grandmother's house one day—it had to be Sunday—when my cousin Mike produced a skateboard. Now neither I nor my brother had been on one of these things, but we had seen some in the stores. Mike talked me into trying it out, and we went to the end of the street to begin. My grandmother's house was on the corner of the street where she lived and the one that continued up the hill. Mike placed one foot on the board and told me to put my foot on it too. I was a little unsure, but I trusted my cousin, so when he pushed off, I grabbed his arm, and down the hill we went. I wasn't sure how we were going to stop when we got to the bottom, but we did. Wouldn't you know it—the Slovak church was letting out. I know many people saw us, and they knew exactly who was on the board. Naturally, when I got home, I was expected to explain the phone call Dad had gotten.

We had relatives in the next town, and when the ones from New Jersey came up, we went to visit them. We all got together in the game room, and my brother and I would watch as the grown-ups would play penny-ante poker. We weren't allowed to play then. We had to grow a little before they would let us.

And of course, when people from away come to Maine, there has to be the ever-popular lobster feed. Back then the lobsters were relatively inexpensive, and you could buy quite a few for a decent price. Clams and corn on the cob rounded out the meal, and everyone had a wonderful time. Boy, those are great memories.

All too soon, vacation time was over, and my relatives had to return to their homes. It was the Sunday before school started, and my brother and I had to be up at five in the morning to catch the bus.

CHAPTER 4

On Lisbon Ridge, when people say it gets dark up there, they are serious. With no street lights and very little traffic on Route 9, when the sun goes down and the dooryard isn't lit up by the light next to the door, the night becomes what is known by all of the residents as D—Dark. On the farm, you could stand on the lawn and not be able to see your hand in front of your face. And if you shined a flashlight down into the field behind the house, you would see the eyes of the deer shining back at you. The best thing about living in the country was when the Northern Lights started; there was no other light to interfere. They would travel through the night sky and shine with a green, ghostly light. It wasn't often they would make it all the way this far south, but when they did, it was magical.

Living down in the village, people get used to having some kind of lighting. Just like the big cities all over the country, there is always a light on— street lights, store signs, traffic lights, even beacons on towers. All around and everywhere, there are lights. I wonder what the power bill is. Everyone is so used to being able to see that when they travel

15

out into the rural areas and there are just no lights, they are intimidated by the dark. It is a darkness that can bring visions of ghosts and goblins even if it isn't Halloween yet.

Living in the country, when I said it was dark out, I meant it. Back at the farm we walked down the driveway and counted the steps to make sure we hadn't walked into the road. One cold, dark morning when we had reached the end, something was blocking the end. We couldn't tell what it was until we heard a loud *moo*. One of the farmer's cows had gotten loose and was eating the grass at the end of our drive. Of course, Jim and I were surprised. I was so surprised I dropped my school books. The cows must have been there a while because my books landed in a cow pie. There was no way I was going to pick them up, and neither was Jim. So we just sat there on the rock wall until the school bus arrived. The driver pulled up, opened the door, and called out, "Is anyone there?"

"Pull up a little more so we can get in," I said. When we got to school and I went to my first class the teacher asked me where my books were. I told him they were lying at the end of our driveway in a pile of manure. Dad had to pay for those books.

There was more than one farmer on the ridge that had cows. I was at my friend's house when we saw the neighbor's cows were loose. We didn't have time to round them up, but we noticed the next-door neighbor's garage, had been invaded by a few of the cows. So we just kind of led the front one to the garage and the rest followed. No one knew who put the cows in the garage, but the owner had a lot to say about it. He also never left his garage door open after that either.

We had a neighbor who lived just down the road from us who had horses. Sometimes some would get loose and find their way up to our fields. One day his horses wandered into our field, and I went out to see what was going on. The next thing I knew, the owner was there yelling at me. At that time, I went back into the house to get Dad's gun. I then went back out and confronted our neighbor. I told him to get his horses and go back home. Just then, Dad drove into the yard and asked me what was going on. The local police also drove into the yard right behind Dad. When Dad asked them what the problem was, the officer said that our neighbor was being threatened by Dad's daughter. After asking a few questions, Dad explained the situation to the officer and told him that his daughter would never shoot anybody. We always had a problem with this one neighbor. It was either his cows or horses that were always finding their way into our fields.

Chapter 5

There are always, little adventures in our lives that don't take up a lot of room in a book but are still kind of funny. My brother and I were very close. Having no one within a quarter of a mile to call a friend, my brother became my best friend. We had our disagreements along with the adventures, but we seemed to work things out. One afternoon, we were in the apple orchard—what we called the line of old apple trees next to the woods. Jim and I had climbed up the oldest tree and were just sitting and talking when he said something that upset me. Being fairly angry, I climbed down, grabbed the ladder, and took it with me as I headed home. Yes, I left my brother up in the tree.

It was supper time, and when Dad, Mom, and I sat down at the table, Dad asked me if I knew where Jim was. I said I did. Dad then suggested that I go get him. I went to the barn, got the ladder, and went back to the tree and put the ladder up so Jim could get down. It had been only a couple of hours since I had left him. When Jim had reached the ground, he explained to me that leaving him in the tree was not a very nice thing to do. When we got back to the house

I was combing the hay and leaves out of my hair—I had waist-length hair then—Dad said, "I see you've found your brother."

We had a well house that sat just a few yards from the back door of our house. It had been built when Mom and Dad hauled water for the farm animals. Every year in the spring, a big black snake would crawl out of the well house and lie on the gravel drive, sunning himself. He would be lying there when Jim and I left for school, so we had to make a wide circle around him. He would always be gone when we got home, but we knew he would be out there again in the morning. We finally named him Magillacuty. That old snake came out and sunned himself for many years. Finally, we didn't see him anymore and we thought he must have died.

We also had a woodchuck living out on the hill in front of the house. He would come out, stand up, and check out the vicinity in case there were enemies about. You know how a woodchuck lives: he has a front door and a back door for escaping. One day, my mother was walking out in front of the house and found Chucky's back door. Chucky was the woodchuck's name. Mom went right up to her hip into Chucky's back door. I don't know how long it took her to get out of the hole, but when Jim and I got home from school, we saw Mom with the rifle, looking for our pet woodchuck, Chucky. Jim said he would get the rifle from Mom and get her into the house, and I was to check on Chucky. Chucky was okay because we saw him the next morning in his old place, looking around. Mom never liked Chucky very much. She would say that he would climb up on the cellar door, look through the window, and sneer at her.

One day, when we were older and I was able to go horseback riding with my best friend, we rode up to my house to get a drink of water. Pauline had only one halter and saddle, so she and I had to ride double. We tied the horse out back and went into the house. I guess Lady thought we had spent enough time in the house. Somehow, she got loose and made her way to the back window. There she stood, looking in and when Ma looked out, she saw an animal looking right back at her. Of course, Ma didn't think this very funny, and she yelled at me to get that horse away from the window. Pauline and I went out back, got on the horse, and rode back down to Pauline's house to put Lady back in the barn. We didn't even have to guide her. She knew the way home, so she just went.

The next exciting day to come along was Halloween. Mom dressed us in our costumes, and we went trick-or-treating in the few houses on the ridge that gave out candy. The weather was getting cold that time of year, and people were burning leaves in their gardens. The smell of the smoke is something I will never forget. Burning leaves beside the road was a popular pastime for the people who lived in town. There was no way to get rid of the leaves when they fell, so the people would rake them to the side of the road and burn them. They would burn a little, and when these turned to ashes, they would add a little more. It turned out to be almost a fall ritual to burn leaves.

Chapter 6

When Dad came home from the war, it wasn't long before he took over as coach of the town ball team. The team's name was the Roberts 88s, and was made up of all local talent. My brother was the bat boy for the team. They were an excellent team and went on to play in the finals in Connecticut. Jim, Mom, and I went along to support the team. We were enjoying the ride when I heard Dad say to the players, "There are kids on this bus, boys." The players had gotten out a deck of cards and were playing poker, but Dad didn't think it was such a good idea.

Mom, Dad, Jim, and I were walking down a street in Connecticut on the day of the game. As we passed a person who had a shoe-shining business, I told Jim I wanted my shoes shined. He looked sideways at me and said, "You've got sneakers on, keep walking." I had never seen a person of color before.

Dad had always loved sports. When he was in high school, he played every game there was—baseball, basketball, football, they were the things that were important. Even in college, he played, and when he enlisted in the army, he organized a team and went fifteen and zero for the season. In college, he set the record for the most triples in one season and held it for fifty years. I finally was able to get him into the Maine Baseball Hall of Fame.

At the age of eight, my friend and I decided to wallpaper the outhouse with the Sears catalog. We cut all of the pages out and pasted and stapled them to the walls. The outhouse was a two-holer, and we thought it looked rather lovely when we were done. It also made reading the catalog a lot easier.

Up overhead in the carriage house, Dad stored a sleigh. He never had the opportunity to take the family for a ride in the winter, but it did make a satisfactory home for brand-new kittens. It seemed we always had a sufficient supply of cats around our barn. Dad would wait until Jim and I were asleep before he would reduce the population of cats. It also worked when the number of chickens would seem lower when I checked on them in the coop. Dad always blamed the reduction on the foxes around the farm.

Everyone in town will remember that November in 1963. It was the month that President Kennedy was assassinated, it was also the month our farm was set on fire by a local pyromaniac. The town of Lisbon had been experiencing numerous fires that fall. More than twenty were fought in the first half of the month, and the whole town was on edge, wondering where the next one would be. Little did we know that it was one of the firemen of the town who was setting them.

We were going to travel to Massachusetts to celebrate my sister's birthday and Thanksgiving. The car was loaded and ready. We were all sound asleep when Mom heard rocks hitting the bedroom window. She looked out and saw the barn all ablaze. She woke Dad up and told him the barn was on fire. It had burned through the outer buildings and was at the house by the time we got out. The Jordan family down the road had seen the flames and had come up to see if they could help. It was lucky they did because if they hadn't woken Mom up, we all would have died. They even pushed Dad's car down into the lower field so it wouldn't blow up. We lost almost all of our belongings in that fire—precious pictures, clothes, toys, and furniture that was in the house. Dad had allowed people to put some things in the barn for storage. There was an old truck, a boat, the uniforms of the ball team that Dad coached, our brand-new bicycles, and other farm equipment were lost. Although Christmas was still a month away, the gifts that had been bought early were also lost. It would be a small Christmas that year, but we were still all together and we thanked God for that. Dad had let some people store their belongings in the barn along with the ball team's uniforms and equipment. Everything was lost in the fire and Mom and Dad had to pay the people out of the insurance money. The town's merchants helped replace the uniforms and equipment, and we were thankful for that.

We had to ask my grandparents if we could live in their house down in town while ours was rebuilt.

Grandpa and Grandma Reid were living in New Jersey with my Aunt Eleanor. This was a whole new world for my brother and me. The house was on the corner of Main Street and Maple Street, right across from the fire department. Whenever a call came in; we had a wonderful show when the trucks left and came back.

Living in town was strange but exciting. Jim and I had to get used to looking both ways when we crossed the road to avoid getting run over. On one side of Main Street, there was Bauer's bakery, a clothing store, a grocery store, and a movie theater. Naturally, we only saw these places when Mom and Dad were shopping. We loved living in town those few months. When we walked down the street, we could smell the fresh bread and cookies from the bakery. We would just stand there, wishing Mom would take us in. Other errands seemed more important.

When a family friend died, Dad bought a riding lawnmower from the estate. He brought it home and showed us how to run it. At this time, we were old enough to be able to mow the lawn. We had been using a push mower, and suddenly being able to ride and mow was a whole new adventure. We had no problem mowing the lawn now and even fought over who would do the chore that day. When we had mowed everything around us, we then went into the field and made circles and paths all the way to the tree line. Dad came home after working all day, saw the fields, and said only one thing: "Did you run out of things to do today?" That was the only thing he said about the fields that day.

The driveway for the farm ran up from the ridge road to the house, where it turned in a circle and reconnected on the other side of the big willow tree. This put the tree right in the middle of the dooryard. It was a big old tree, and the limbs were so long they dragged on the ground. When we mowed the lawn with the push mower, they weren't much of a problem because one of us would hold the limbs up while the other mowed. But with the riding mower, it was too dangerous to hold the limbs while the mower went by, so I got Dad's trimming shears out and gave that old tree a haircut. I cut the limbs about five feet from the ground, and after that, it wasn't a problem to mow the lawn. Dad never said a word about the tree.

One day, Dad told Jim and me to choose what church we were going to attend. My family was catholic at this time. My grandparents had left Czechoslovakia in 1901, had met on the boat coming to America, and had gotten married in New Jersey when they arrived. So we worshiped in the Slovak church. When I reached the age when everyone was expected to go to confession, I had a problem. Why did I have to confess to something when I had done nothing bad that week? I told the priest that I could get into trouble myself without making something up. When Dad dropped us off at the church the next Sunday, Jim and I walked to the Methodist church down the street. When the service was over, we met Dad back at the Catholic Church.

All the years going to the Catholic Church, I, along with the other parishioners would celebrate Ash Wednesday. It meant a day off from school for the children. When Jim and I went to the Methodist church, we still celebrated Ash Wednesday with the Catholics. We would leave school, go to the church, have the ashes put on our foreheads, and spend the rest of the day in town. This practice ended, though, when my English teacher was hired to play the organ at the Methodist church. Jim and I just couldn't get away with celebrating with the other church anymore. Oh well.

Halloween was a lot more fun because there were a lot more homes to visit, which meant more candy. It was fun seeing all the other kids in their costumes, running from one house to another, yelling "Trick or treat". When we had visited all of the houses Mom wanted to take us to, we looked into our treat bags and found enough candy to last until Christmas. It was a good thing I had a dentist for an uncle.

Thanksgiving and Christmas were exciting because the relatives came to celebrate with us. The town was decorated with lights and the storefronts showed all kinds of gifts that could be bought. Downtown was alive with shoppers looking for just the right gift and going from store to store. Living on the ridge, we only saw the lights that the neighbors put up. But living in town, every neighborhood was lit up. Dad would load everyone into the car, and we would ride around the town looking at all of the houses.

In the afternoon, when the workers left the mill, they would walk up the street and do their shopping for the day. Then, after supper, they would come back and do their Christmas shopping. Back then, people didn't have to leave the town to shop. We had everything we needed, from groceries to furniture.

The school was a whole different experience living in town. We could walk to school and we didn't have to worry about cows being in the driveway. There were a lot more kids to walk to school with, and some of them lived right up the hill from us. My brother and I had a lot more to do when we were in town. In the summers, we played ball and any other kind of game at the school.

Nineteen sixty-nine was a year of firsts for our country. We had a rock concert take place in Massachusetts that lasted three days and was attended by thousands of young people. It was days of music, drugs, and hunger. The organizers were overwhelmed by the number of attendees. I wonder what it was like.

It was the year when we, as a country, achieved what our President challenged us to do: put a man on the moon. We actually put two there and brought them back.

One winter day, I and a friend went to the old high school to skate. The town always flooded the area behind the school so the kids—and the parents, too—would have a place to skate. I was skating along when this older boy went by, pulling some others in what we called a "whip." The last kid in line grabbed my hand, and off we went. Well, the boy up front turned suddenly and "snapped" the whip. I, being on the end, was propelled into the nearest snowbank. When the boy realized what had happened, he came over to where I was struggling to get out of the snowbank and helped me. He asked me if I was alright and then skated off with his friends. Whenever I was able to go skating, I would see him.

Chapter 7

In the spring of 1970, I was down in town with my brother, looking for something to do. A few of the local boys had talked the town into letting them use the basement of the library as a place to practice their music. They had formed a small band and needed a place to keep their equipment and had cleaned the place up. The town officials gave them permission with the understanding that if any problems were caused by allowing other kids to enter, the area would revert to a storage area, and the band would have to find another place to practice. For a few years, the rules were followed and the basement became known as "The Shelter." It wasn't open to other kids until the weekend when other fledgling bands would come in to play. The kids had salvaged couches and chairs and had built a kind of stage to play on. There was no food or soda provided, so if you wanted a pizza, you had to buy your own. Mostly, the kids behaved themselves until some kids from other towns heard about "The Shelter" and came to see what it was all about. When that began, it was the beginning of the end for "The Shelter." The town closed it down when drugs came onto the scene.

I was just starting to walk up to the high school, where Dad was the moderator of that year's town meeting when the boy who had put me into the snowbank a few years earlier came along. He had his dad's car and asked me if I needed a ride home. I didn't want to wait for my dad to finish the meeting, as it would be quite late, so I said yes. I jumped in and asked to be taken to the high school so I could let my dad know I had a ride home. I learned the name of the boy after he helped me out of the snowbank. His name was Don. He played the trumpet in the school band, and when I entered the eighth grade, I also played in the band. I played the flute.

We got to the school, and Don went with me so I could introduce him to my dad. After meeting Don, Dad was ok with him giving me a ride home. We got to my house, and Don asked me if he could see me again. I said yes, jumped out of the car, and ran into the house. When Dad got home, he said just one thing to me: "Don't get serious." That was all.

I couldn't see him during the week, but he would always call to ask me out on the weekend. He would come to the farm, and we would sit and talk, or we would ride into town and spend a few hours with friends at the local pizza shop. Summers were for hiking the fields and woods. Fall was for picking apples, raking leaves, helping my best friend bale hay and stack the bales in the barn, and watching TV. Don had a portable TV that he would bring to the farm and would sit in the living room and watch. Most evenings would end at nine o'clock.

High school was a place to learn the basic tools that we, as up-and-coming adults, would need to succeed in life. It was also a place to make friends and have a lot of fun if you could get away with it.

The school had a band, as I mentioned in a previous chapter. I played flute, and my brother played trumpet. There were concerts we would practice for and other occasions where we were asked to perform. And for a few years, we even played at the local football games.

There was one concert we played where we traveled to Upper Maine. The school chartered a bus and loaded everyone on with their luggage and instruments. It was quite a trip to Deer Isle. We left on a Friday and returned on Sunday. Everything went well, and everyone enjoyed the time away from home and parents. The real memories are from the next weekend when Deer Isle's band came here for a concert. Like us, they arrived Friday and returned home Sunday. It was the party on Friday evening that made the best memories. I don't remember how many band members came down, but they all stayed at the local motel. After practice, plans were made to meet at my farm and have a party. Things were going well; everyone was behaving themselves. (There was no drinking, as none of us were old enough to buy beer.) But when it got to be overly late, one of the band directors arrived with a bullhorn and pleasantly explained that anyone not found at the motel in twenty minutes would not enjoy the ride home. You never saw so many kids load up the cars so fast. My brother and I loaded eight or nine other people into my dad's Javelin and headed for the motel. There were arms and legs sticking out of every window. We made it, though, and no one got into any trouble. The concert was a success, and we made many wonderful friends.

Winter was sliding, skating, shoveling and just staying inside where it was warm. Sometimes Don and I would put puzzles together at my house, and other times we would go to his house and walk around the park, looking at the houses and talking. Whenever we were in town, we had to be careful not to embarrass my dad. He was a selectman, and if we did anything off-color, the people who knew me would be right on the phone with Mom. We both understood, so we were always careful just to hold hands when we were together. Don said he had no problem with my request.

Don's mom worked at Pineland Hospital in Powell. His dad had suffered a stroke and had lost his voice. Don stayed home while his mom worked and took care of his dad. His mom worked the second shift, and he had to take her to work at three o'clock in the afternoon and go get her at eleven o'clock at night. His dad would ride with him just to get out of the house. This was their routine for two years, and then his mom retired. Don still had to stay home because he was the only one who had a driver's license. His mom and dad relied on him to do whatever errands needed to be done.

We would go out on weekends when I could get a Saturday off, but most of the time, I had to work. I had gotten a job at the local discount drugstore and went right to work after school. Don was working in the mill at the time on the third shift. He would pick me up at 9:00 p.m. and take me home. Then he would go home and rest until it was time for him to go in. Don worked until his dad died on a Saturday morning in the spring of 1970. From then on, he had to stay around home to care for his mom.

CHAPTER 8

We dated for two years, and then one fall afternoon, Don asked me what size ring I wore. I was in my third year of high school then, but I had an idea where this was going. He had bought what was then called a pre-engagement ring. It was dark gold with one white pearl and one black pearl. On a Saturday or Sunday afternoon in the fall of 1970, he asked me to wear it. We were together through 1971 and 1972, and on Christmas Eve 1972, Don asks me to marry him and he gave me a diamond ring. I could hardly say a word, but I did get "Yes" out. It took almost the rest of the evening to get my voice back. His cousin was there and was struck speechless. From then on, we spent most of our time planning our wedding. I had been saving money, and so had Don. We wanted to help our parents as much as we could with the expenses of a small wedding. My dad asked me just one thing in all of this time. He said, "Are you sure this is what you want?" I said, "Yes." That was all.

One late spring Saturday, about eleven thirty in the morning, Don drove into the dooryard at the farm. He got out of the car and stood still for a few moments, curious about the voices he heard. He started to walk around the house, calling my name. I yelled to come back in an hour. He wanted to know what the problem was and I yelled again, "Just come back in an hour." He said, "Okay," and got back into his car and drove off. Just as he was leaving, my dad pulled up to the house. He had gone inside the house and had asked Mom if she had seen the navy helicopter flying overhead. He was wondering why they kept circling. Dad asked Mom if she had heard anything about a possible wood fire. Mom told him, "For goodness' sake, Amel, the girls are sunbathing up on the roof." Dad then yelled for us to put our clothes on and get down here for lunch. Don came back a little later, and we all had a good laugh.

Another Saturday, my friend Pauline and I wanted to wash our hair—not with shampoo and water, but with beer. The big thing back then was to use beer; it was supposed to do something special for your hair. After popping open one beer, we decided it wasn't doing anything for our hair, so why waste it? We drank it instead. Pauline then got the idea to look for her old roller skates in the barn. I had never been on roller skates before, but it sounded like fun. After a few beers, anything would sound like fun. We got back to my house, and I succeeded in getting the skates on. I then went down to the road and tried to skate back to Pauline's house. While I was skating along the centerline of the road, my dad went by going in the other direction and headed to the house. I yelled to Pauline that I thought it was Dad who just went by. We made it to Pauline's, took off the skates, put them back in the barn, and headed home. When I got there, Dad was a little upset.

He asked me, "What were you thinking roller-skating down the middle of Route 9 two weeks before your wedding? Do you want to get married with no teeth?"

Calmly I said, "Do you see any sidewalks?" That was the only time I left Dad speechless.

Well, the day of my wedding came. It started fairly quiet, but the weather was never going to cooperate. The humidity flowed in, and the mesh hats the girls wore wilted down around their faces. That was the first issue. Things continued well, and everyone arrived at the church in plenty of time. At the specified time, the music started, Dad walked me down the aisle, and Don and I stood in front of the minister. We had two ministers at our wedding. Ms. Nellie Lane had been the minister before the one doing the service and she came back just to help at mine. Reverend Twiddy started off well, but when he came to the line, "Do you," he was supposed to say Donald, he said David. I, being ready for anything, spoke out loud enough for the back of the church to hear: "His name is Donald." It was a good thing I said that because some of the guests were beginning to wonder if I had the right guy. Well, the minister was quick enough to realize his mistake and revised his question, and Donald and I were married on June 30, 1973, at eleven thirty in the morning. It was the minister's very first wedding.

The rest of the day went as it was supposed to, I and my new husband stayed at the appropriate time at the reception, and we hoped everyone had fun after we left on our honeymoon. The funny thing is, we don't remember what was served for the meal. What does that tell you?

We had made reservations at the motel on Bailey Island for the next two days, so we headed down to the ocean to spend the first night. My dad and mom had bought me a beautiful nightgown to wear, but when I put it on and turned my back to the wall heater, I put a few discolored marks on the back. That was the first night of our life together.

# CHAPTER 9

I thought I would add a few of the more interesting adventures I had early in my marriage. Don and I had found an apartment the year before we got married. It was brand-new. One of the local businessmen in town had started building low-income housing in Lisbon. So far, there have been three new buildings, and we were able to acquire the last one in the newest building. It was an upstairs, four-room apartment and quite nice. We spent the year moving in pieces of furniture we purchased. We found a nice bedroom set at the local trading post, and Don's mom gave us a kitchen table, chairs, and an old couch she wasn't using. We didn't move in until after we were married. We settled into married life easily. I worked days and Don worked the third shift at the mill. He worked in the dye house, and his clothes were all colors. He had to use the bathroom to change his clothes. He would stand in the tub so the dye would go down the drain and then take a shower to wash it off.

Summer was fun. We would spend time with my mom and dad on the farm and Don's mom at her house in town. When fall came, the leaves turned the most vivid colors. The farm looked like a painting, and Don's mom had the prettiest red maple I ever saw.

I missed most of the fall because I wasn't well. Dad took me to the local doctor, and he told me I had to have my tonsils out. I tried to talk my way out of it, but Dad wouldn't listen. The day was scheduled, and I didn't expect to be in the hospital for more than two or three days. I had asked the doctor if I could continue taking my pill and was told it would be fine. Dad and Don took me to the hospital, and the operation went okay. My throat was sore, and all I wanted to eat was ice cream, but I did go home after three days. I went back to the farm so my mom could care for me while Don worked at night. He would go to our apartment to clean up and then he joined me at the farm. It wasn't long, though, before I started to experience pain in my left leg. I had gotten well enough not to have to stay in bed, but now I had pain in my throat and leg. Dad took me back to the doctor, and he told Dad to get me back to the hospital immediately. The problem was a blood clot that had formed when I was under anesthesia for the tonsil operation. I had cold compresses on my throat for the pain and hot ones on my leg for the clot. I don't understand why the doctor said I was a difficult patient. He should have been in my shoes, so to speak. Do you think I was unreasonable when my stay in the hospital went from three days to eleven weeks?

Don and I lived in the apartment for one year. When we moved in, the owner told us not to pound nails into the walls. He wanted us to use the adhesive hangers. They were okay unless you wanted to hang any kind of picture. Those hangers did more damage than any nail. They would work for about a couple hours and then they would pull the sheetrock paper right off.

I had only one large problem while we were living there. The family downstairs had a little boy. He got a trike for his birthday and he would ride it all over the apartment. It was a little annoying, but when he started to run it into the cupboards, it would cause many a cake to fall. If I wanted to bake a cake, I would have to go back to the farm. It was rather aggravating. The one problem that was kind of funny was the reaction of our neighbor to my mantel clock. We didn't hear anything about it until one weekend evening when the couple loudly stated, "There goes that damn clock again." Don went right to the clock and stopped it. It hasn't run since. It was when we returned home from grocery shopping and witnessed a fight going on right in front of our door that I told Don I thought it was time to find a house and move.

CHAPTER 10

In early 1974, we started looking for a home. We drove around town to see if there were any "For Sale" signs—there weren't many. We then went to see the local real estate broker, but he had only a few in town. We looked at them, but they weren't quite what we were looking for. It looked like we might have to move out of town, but then we heard of a house that had just come onto the market

It was January 1975, and I was painting the bathroom. We had an old iron bathtub with claw feet, and I had gotten down on my knees to paint behind it. I was carrying my first baby at the time and was a little big. It was a good thing my dad checked on me three or four times a day because I had gotten stuck and couldn't back out. Dad had to pull me out by my feet. He told me to wait a few more months before I started redecorating anything else. Matt was born on March 9, 1975. I was in the hospital for three days after Matt was born. The food at the hospital was rather dull, and I so wanted some French fries. We decided we would stop at the McDonald's on the way home. That was how Matt visited McDonald's when he was three days old.

The first year with our new son was a learning curve for both of us. Matt was a happy baby but always hungry. Don and I would make up six bottles of formula in the morning before we went to work. Don's mom looked after Matt then. He would work his way through the bottles and would have just enough left to have one for supper. We would make six more for the night. As he grew, I had to add a little rice cereal to the formula to fill him up. When he graduated to baby food, he couldn't get enough Blueberry Buckle. It's funny that he loved all of the veggies but when he passed onto solid food, I couldn't get him to eat anything green.

Matt, being the first arrival, was the center of attention for about two years. His grandparents adored him and would spoil him at every visit. That little boy had been taken to every meeting my dad attended during the day. The night meetings lasted too late into the night. When Dad was at the town office and in a meeting with the other selectmen, the girls in the office would look after Matt until the meeting was over.

When Matt was one, my dad died. It was Christmas Eve, 1975. Then six months later, in the spring of 1976, Mom died. That was a very hard time for me.

It was that winter when my brother and sister decided to sell the farm. Don and I would have liked to buy it, but we had just bought our own house and had no idea how we could afford it. It was late winter, and you could feel spring in the air. The snow was starting to melt, and the days were bright and sunny. My sister found a real estate broker who agreed to sell the farm for us, but he wanted to see the property lines. I would take snowshoes to walk the lines, and Don and I had experience, but the broker didn't. Nope, none at all. I was carrying my next child when we strapped on the snowshoes and headed out through the fields. The broker did well until we got into the trees. It wound up being a comedy of errors, but we all made it back to the house with no mishaps.

Matt's brother, David, came along just when we were getting ready for Christmas of 1977. We had a devil of a time when he was little, explaining that Santa brought toys to all the children, not just him. December was a little bit hectic when he came along. Of course, his brother was a little upset at the change in his status, but he grew to love his brother.

The Christmas of 1978 was one we remember well. Matt was three, and David was just one. We were all asleep—or so I thought—when I heard something downstairs. I got up and went to see what the noise was. Matt had gotten up and went down to look at the tree. The noise I heard was him unwrapping all of the gifts, and I mean all. He had unwrapped everything and was walking around with one K-Tel plastic ski that his grandmother had bought him. I took him back to bed and spent the next three hours putting the tree back together. I was in tears, using all of the tape—including masking tape.

Both of the little boys had a wonderful Christmas. Our tree was surrounded by gifts from the whole family. I think maybe we spoiled the boys a little.

Our boys were the average boys in any town. They would ride their bikes and play ball. They had friends, and both of them played an instrument in the school band. Their dad would take them fishing and would talk to them about camping. They both loved to go to L.L. Bean in Freeport, just to walk around and look at the camping equipment. We had a woodstove, and we would show them how to cut and stack the firewood. They loved sitting next to the fire and watching the snow come down. Actually, we all loved the woodstove. When their dad would start the stove for the first time in late fall, they knew Halloween wasn't far away. We burned wood for thirty-five years, and the boys never got tired of splitting and stacking the wood. The best times were when the power went out. We would light the stove and set up the oil lamps for when it got dark. Those were the times when the cribbage board would come out. They were always hoping the power would go out.

❧

CHAPTER 11

In 1998, the state of Maine experienced a once-in-a-lifetime storm. It wasn't very cold, and it started out as rain. The temperature began to drop, and when the rain entered the cold air, it froze. The ice collected on the trees and power lines up to a quarter of an inch thick, which was heavy enough to bring whole limbs down and break some poles. There were even numerous transformers that shorted and blew. The state of Maine and surrounding other states were without power, sometimes for weeks at a time. We had twenty-eight people staying in our house for two weeks.

When the boys were old enough, they joined the Little League baseball teams. Matt's first team was the Tigers. They were undefeated, and the league retired the whole team's shirts.

The boys both learned to play instruments. Matt played the trumpet, and David played the tenor saxophone. Both boys played well enough to be accepted at the Maine Music Festival. When the town organized a community band, they and their father played in it.

The boys stayed with their grandmother when Don and I went to work. When they were small, she would let Matt watch TV while she rocked David. Then she would hold Matt while David slept in his crib. Grandma loved those boys to death, but she loved all little ones also. That is why she took Don and his sister into her house when they were small, as their own parents couldn't care for them. All the way up until the boys were able to look after themselves, they stayed with Grandma. She would make breakfast for them—pancakes, French toast, or scrambled eggs were on the menu every day. Grandma had an empty lot next to her house. Over the years wild blueberries and strawberries had taken root. The boys would pick enough blueberries for Grandma to make muffins.

In all of those years, we had almost as many adventures as I did growing up. We even had a few broken bones, which is something I never experienced, thank God! Don and I have been married for forty-seven years now. They have been nothing if not interesting. We have two boys who were lively and entertaining right from the start.

One afternoon, early in our marriage, Don asked me why I married him. After thinking about his question for a few minutes, I told him. I said, "Because you were polite." We still chuckle about that.

I hope our lives will continue to be filled with happiness, as they have been so far. We have lived as well as we could and have made many friends who have become our extended family. We know someday they will have their own lives to live and the "family" will get smaller and smaller as the years go by. But that's life. My sons always come "home" on the holidays and they visit almost every weekend they can. As their father grows older, they say they will come over to help him take care of the old "homestead." I hope they do.

APPENDIX

A Thought from the Husband

In June of 2018, I wrote a poem for Jane for our anniversary. When I had finished it, I was unsure how she would feel about it, so I let her read it. I wanted to read it in church on our anniversary, but she said no. I had planned a small party for her, so I put it with the cards so other people could read it. I add it here as an addendum.

God's Plan

On a sunny winter day, right from the start,
When I pulled you from the snowbank, you captured
    my heart.
Little did we know, when I took your hand,
That God was making for us a better plan.
We dated a few others and took our time,
But I kept thinking as the days passed,
About making you mine.

I saw you in town one cool, rainy night.
And asked you if you needed a ride home. You said,
    "Alright."
From there, we moved slowly, not wanting to rush.
We kept things quiet so the parents wouldn't fuss.
One year went by, and we were still a couple.
There was fun and laughter and only a little trouble.
The second year ran along well, and the holidays
    were fine.
Christmas arrived and I asked you to be mine.
I gave you a ring and said, "Let's set a date."
You, being the sensible one, said, "I think we should
    wait."
We were married on the last day of June.
There was no one more nervous when I heard that
    wedding tune.
The minister had his next event running in his head.
When he asked, "Do you, David?", "His name is
    Donald," you loudly said.
The years crept by, and we had two sons.
Both were perfect, we got the best ones.
Through the years, we have been happy and sad.
We have made many friends, and we have lost Mom
    and Dad.
We stayed together and held up each other,
Especially when you lost your twin brother.
We worked side by side, in and out of the house,
But I being from town, you got rid of the mouse.
It's been forty-plus years, and God's plan has worked
    for us.
I made you mine because God said I must.

There was no way to argue, and I heartily agree,
That "you and I" finally became "we.".
When we have come to the end of our road,
When we can stop and rest and put down our load,
I will wait before the gates no matter the weather,
And we will walk through them arm and arm
together.

(D. G. Wile 2018)

ABOUT THE AUTHOR

Growing up in a small town, my life had a few challenges, but I learned to be self-sufficient. Being mostly alone, I turned to reading. I fell in love with books and would spend my spare time reading anything that had to do with science fiction. I did learn to play a musical in school, which led me unknowingly to my future wife. That was far in the future. I started writing small stories in grad school but never thought I might write something people would like to read. In English class, we had to write book reports and essays on popular authors. I had to do one on Lousia May Alcott five times before I got it right.

In high school, every year, a term paper was required. Writing became almost as important as reading, and in my senior year, I succeeded in achieving an A+ on the last one I wrote. There was no money for college, so I went to work in the local mill. I worked the third shift, so writing kind of took a back seat. It wasn't until I had been married for quite a few years that I started writing in earnest. Poems were in the beginning and then short stories. I started a book, but it wasn't until the year 2000 that I began this book. Before I could submit it though, my wife had to read it and make the changes to keep it correct. I hope you will find it interesting at the least. All of the stories actually happened.

www.ingramcontent.com/pod-product-compliance
Lightning Source LLC
Chambersburg PA
CBHW061409140726

47997CB00003B/1437